JOHN THOMPSON
"Do you like 'em then?"

Published by Clark Art Ltd 2006
www.clark-art.co.uk

© Copyright **ClarkArt**Ltd

Photographs of paintings by Clive Good.

ISBN 0-9552591-0-X
ISBN 0-9552591-1-8 (limited edition 100 copies)

Acknowledgements:

We would like to thank everyone who helped in the
production of this book. Special mention is due to the
following individuals:

Charles Barker, Jo Bennett, John Buckley, Chris Chapman,
Julia Cox & Colin Frost, Claire Curtis-Thomas, Michael Dunn,
Clive Good, Jenny Knight, Wendy Momen, Diane Nobilio,
Maureen Sandiford, and last but not least
John and Shirley Thompson.

JOHN THOMPSON

"Do you like 'em then?"

By Stuart Archer
and Bill Clark

Golden Forest - Detail

Contents

Foreword

I first came across John Thompson's work in a gallery in Whitefield in 2001. At this time I was still more of a picture collector than a dealer and I was in the process of building up a collection of works by northern artists such as L.S. Lowry, Adolphe Valette, Helen Bradley, Theodore Major and Alan Lowndes.

When I first saw John's Group Series paintings they had an instant impact on me. They were very northern in feel - groups of men in flat caps against empty backgrounds, yet the paintings had a haunting quality about them and I was particularly drawn to the expressions on the characters' faces. I also noted that none of the painting had titles, they had just been given numbers, so you were left to make your own mind up about what was going on. Over the next year or so I bought about a dozen of his works for my own collection, little did I realise that five years later I would be representing John Thompson and producing a book about him.

John is a larger than life character who loves meeting the people who buy his paintings, he is always interested to find out what they think of his work. He is a prolific painter, even though he is now in his 80's he is still very disciplined and spends 5 afternoons a week in his studio painting. It's hard to believe he has produced over 2000 Group Series paintings.

A visit to his studio in Greenfield is an adventure, it's like an Aladdin's cave, there are hundreds of unframed paintings stored in browsers and dozens of framed works stacked against the walls, you don't know what you are going to find next - fantastic Group Series paintings, vibrant still lifes, risqué nudes, complex abstracts or humorous black and white sketches. It's an exciting visual experience for anyone who visits and coupled with John's on-going commentary it's very hard to come away without buying something.

In recent years John has been very successful, he has a loyal and expanding base of collectors, many of whom I have met whilst doing research for this book. Once people meet John and see the breadth of his work they're hooked and they tend to keep coming back for more.

His paintings seem to connect with people on a very personal level, they often remind them of family members or places they have visited or events which have occurred in their lives. This is totally unintentional on John's part, he is an intuitive painter who doesn't seem to plan his work. Different people will interpret his paintings in different ways for this ambiguity is all part of his magic and makes his work appeal to people of all ages and backgrounds. This book will help bring his work to a wider audience.

Bill Clark, March 2006

John's son Scott in Meldrum Street 1961
Pencil Drawing 8" x 6" Collection of John Thompson

*D*on't you see yourself in every picture you love? You feel a radiance wash through you. It's something you can't analyze or speak about clearly. What are you doing at the moment? You're looking at a picture on a wall. That's all. But it makes you feel alive in the world. It tells you yes, you're here. And yes, you have a range of being that's deeper and sweeter than you knew.'

Don DeLillo: 'Cosmopolis'. 2003

Introduction

*S*prightly octogenarian; wiry; sparky; thinning white hair; warm smile; down to earth - does not stand on ceremony; chuckles at his own stories; casually dressed, often wearing a flat cap.

Voluble; a compulsive talker; graphic memory; raconteur extraordinaire; digresses; confident in his own artistic abilities.

A small studio in Kinders Lane , Greenfield - a Lancashire village in the shadows of the Pennine hills. The studio is packed with paintings stacked haphazardly. The walls are covered with striking examples of his early and recent work. Hardly enough room to swing a cat, but he now has plenty of visitors.

First impressions of a painter to whom success has come late. But how do character and career inform the work of any artist? Does it matter what kind of life he has led?

In the case of John Thompson, the answer is almost certainly yes.

Inside the studio

10

The Earlier Years

A lad with something about him

Born in Salem, Oldham in 1924, John lost his mother when he was only fifteen years old. His father had a formative influence on his youth.

John's parents

John left school at fourteen - his main distinction already was for ability in art classes.

His first job was machine minding at a luggage firm, but an accident almost lost him two fingers and led to more expensive safety precautions, so he was soon 'dispensed with'.

He then worked on the railways for nine years (his father, Bob, was a railway builder). First he was a probationer in the Signal and Telegraph department.. He was a smart lad to whom his elders listened with interest (they wouldn't have had much choice?). He drew in his less productive hours at work, and some of his work was sent to London for appraisal. He was offered a job in the Drawing Office in Manchester.

'You were always changing jobs'

After he left the railways he began to drift. A season in a holiday camp in Blackpool: nine months building transformers for Ferranti.

He was independent. He refused to join the trade unions. He would answer back if he felt he was being treated unfairly. He kept up his interest in art however by attending life drawing classes for five years in the evening, where he impressed because he could already draw a 'nervous', powerful line, and he was offered work in commercial art which he turned down as too boring.

I can't do without her'

He met and married his wife, Shirley, in 1955. They celebrated their golden wedding in 2005 with a cruise on the QE2 (apparently he also made a big splash here as there was a television crew on board). Shirley has done a great deal to promote and publicise his work. Shirley was (and is) a steadying influence. A common-sense counterbalance to his sometimes eccentric enthusiasms, she has prevented him from 'getting carried away'. She has also recorded his successes and encouraged him in his experiments. It was Shirley who took his work to Salford Art gallery and persuaded the curator to give him his first one-man show. She has been the rock on which John leans.

John and Shirley

He went into retail, becoming Display Manager in the Halifax branch of Harrison Gibson, a famous avant garde and expensive furniture shop. He painted pictures to enhance his furniture settings. He soon became well-known, and students from the Percival Whitley College came to copy his window dressings. (He was later to lecture at the College on display techniques). His paintings sold like hot cakes for the equivalent of his weekly wage.

Full-Time Painter

'We had no choice'

I n 1980, aged 56, he was made redundant in the recession. He decided to try to make a living as an independent painter. This was a brave decision but there seemed to be no alternative.

John in his studio at Uppermill

He started in the Corn Exchange Buildings in Hanging Ditch, Manchester. He was always keen to talk about his work and he invited the public to watch him painting. At this stage he was willing to try his hand at anything.

After nine months of slim success, when he only made enough to pay for his calor gas bottle to be refilled, he moved to the Alexandra Craft Centre in Uppermill. He was at rock bottom. He had to sell his car. He had no pension, no grants, no income except for picture sales. Yet he quickly developed a warm rapport with his visitors, stemming perhaps from his long experience in retail. He always liked to meet people and talk to them.

'Well, what shall I paint today?'

He often worked from old photographs supplied by the Council collection of the records of demolished buildings. The older the better, for he sought atmosphere, not exact and precise details, as he strove for the 'history' of a townscape in the style of Valette. He did not copy but compress and simplify - the vertical into the horizontal, and vice versa. He really wanted to sell a picture a day.

'Do you like 'em then?'

He cultivated a 'Joe Bloggs, Andy Capp cloth cap image' as he challenged potential customers for their views of his work, and he soon developed a sense of what would sell. 'People would say to me, "You've stood on the west side of this or that hill and painted such and such a valley". I would say, "Oh, aye". But it was tongue in cheek - I hadn't. It was just that they liked to think they knew the scene and recognised it'.

In 1986 he painted a convincing and lively picture of the Oldham Coliseum Theatre as it had been in Victorian times, with bustling queues and horse-drawn carriages.

Visitors often bought a local landscape as a souvenir and his sales slowly increased. He seemed to be lucky too - whenever a big bill arrived he seemed to find a buyer. Painting had made him independent, but his work was not yet satisfyingly creative.

An early success which brought him publicity was a portrait of Charles and Diana on their engagement. He transformed the stark black and white official photograph into a romantic spring-like image, with flowers and a focus on the engagement ring. It was shown at Earl's Court in London and a print was displayed in the Maples stores.

Brochure featuring John's Painting of Oldham Coleseum Theatre

Charles and Diana

He remembers early customers. A young man who bought a Picasso-style portrait in memory of his father. A young husband who spent the money saved up for a first three piece suite on Christmas Eve on an early group painting instead. (What did his wife say about this?). A successful engineer who bought a series of his groups to decorate his specially built board and reception rooms. He found women usually had a shrewder intuition and appreciation of his work than men.

An early supporter was the art dealer, Jo Bennett. She has been in the business since the 1970s , has wide contacts, and is very well-respected in the national art world. Always warm and welcoming, she bought his work at first as presents for friends and family. She was quick to appreciate his originality, flair, and the freedom with which he worked. Her clientele also quickly responded to his idiosyncrasy and eccentricity. He connects with an eclectic audience, some of whom are sophisticated and erudite, others nostalgic for the fifties and the sixties. Jo began to show his work in exhibitions around the country, promoting him successfully and introducing him to important collectors. The connection continues, to

mutual benefit, as she argues that he has powered his way to success through his paintings.

Another early influence was the wealthy Manchester businessman and art collector, Jack Garson. Garson had framed Lowry's paintings and John took his work there. Most of his collection was Italian, but he had a valuable Holbein. The only contemporary work in the collection was one of John' s groups. He gave shrewd advice on the nuances of the market and had a keen eye for what might have potential.

'Painting is almost day-dreaming. Age brings experience and depth'

In October, 1986 he stumbled by accident upon a personal style, almost a trademark. He looked at an American black and white lithograph of men standing in a soup kitchen queue, in snow in the Bronx.

Fascinated by the group of figures, he decided to isolate them from any background, any environment. 'I didn't want to copy it'. But the removal of context created an elusive mystery.

'People were talking about my figures straight away'

When he took his early groups to Jack Garson for a valuation, he was told that 'these were something different, and things might happen'. Garson told him to stop signing them but simply to initial them with a monogram - 'These paintings are now your signature'. He had found an individual style - he had made a creative breakthrough.

From Manchester to Westminster

The groups were strongly promoted by Elaine Grace (formerly Mather) at her new gallery - the Gallery, Manchester's Art House. Elaine photographed and catalogued his paintings and held two major exhibitions in 2002 and 2004. The 2002 exhibition was sensationally successful; the 2004 was a retrospective to celebrate his eightieth birthday.

A very important step in his national success came with the purchase in 2002 of three of his group series by the Curator of the House of Lords' collection to hang in new Committee offices in the Palace of Westminster. They were seen as an example of the spirit of Manchester and the North West. Publicity exploded with his exposure to regional and national television. A sales explosion also followed quickly. The prestige tickled his pride and reinforced his reputation.

John and Shirley with Simon Carter, Curator, House of Lords

John and Group Series Painting

The Group Series

'We are all filled by our past'

A living artist is open to question. We can learn from him. What does John Thompson tell us about his work?

Discussion of artistic style and development in writing is inevitably a clumsy process. The artist may develop a rationale for his work, but this is hardly his main concern. He may have to think of the future, for his work may well be misunderstood in the present. One of John's earliest patrons, an academic who taught Russian, told him that intelligent collectors in the future would see things in his work that he did not know about. The common comment on his group series is that each group was 'more than the sum of its parts'. They immediately provoked discussion.

When he sets out to capture images of people around him, ordinary people, his contemporaries, he does not plan or premeditate. There is no intrinsic meaning, no didactic purpose, no overt political or social comment. The faces are often (but not always) anonymous, and in painting the groups he is expressing his own sense of personality, an acceptance of himself, a search for self-identification.

In an age of mass media and information technology, the emphasis upon groups and individuals is itself idiosyncratic and rebellious - an escape from the mediocrity of a globalized culture, an idea which challenges the conformity of the common patterns of thought, and the crust of custom.

The removal of the physical environment in most (but not all) of the groups is a stimulus to individuality. Viewers can interpret for themselves and develop their own 'narratives'. The painting is an event, a performance, a happening - it sets a scene in which mystery and enigma dominate. The groups are left untitled so that their apparent aimlessness and lack of purpose is not made specific and so that the essential ambiguity is protected.

Group Series 463 Mixed Media 32"x 44"
Collection of John Thompson

The frequent anonymity of the figures and faces stems from a richness of reference to the impact of the past upon the present. His own experiences are used as a guide - an anchor of memories wrenched slowly and perhaps reluctantly from the sea of consciousness.

Sunday evenings on family visits, when the men went to the pub and he was left behind - fascinated by the pictures in a 24 volume red-bound history of the Great War. Here he saw the men who marched away - the Lancashire Fusiliers in their thousands, with bow legs and knock knees.

He was interested in crowds and the images of crowds - masses of people, in old photographs, seas of faces at football matches, almost indistinguishable.

'Old Photographs'

'Smiles like frozen songs,
Eyes in faces fading,
Still and staring'

(from a poem by John Thompson)

In dealing with groups he faced the perennial problems of complexity and diversity. How to unify them? Issues of light and shade, and of colour. Whether to make them solid and sculptural or flimsy and fragile. Is there a pattern binding the group together? Do they become a unit? How do they react and interact? Is there tension and hostility or comradeship and co-operation? Is colour merely a background or is it an integral element in the design? Is he echoing earlier patterns, or working purely from his own imagination?

Artists have been engaged with and intrigued by such problems for centuries. The Christian tradition created magnificent group paintings of such set-pieces as the nativity, the miracles, the crucifixion and the descent from the cross. The altarpieces of even the humblest Italian village churches might be painted by a Giotto or a Bellini. The First and Second World Wars also proved a rich source for group pictures, from officers and gentlemen to sappers and gassed casualties. The work of Eric Kennington and John Singer Sargent on the Great War and Henry Moore's drawings of Londoners taking shelter in the Underground during the Blitz spring to mind.

John Thompson's originality was to remove the immediate story and to allow the spectator to create his or her own version of the action (or inaction). Theories about artistic purpose are often projections back upon the artist of the effect his work has upon us. Whatever the theory, the group series quickly became very popular.

'Who the hell does he think he is?'

In August 1988 (eight years after setting up independently) he had his first one-man show at Salford Art Gallery. He took 57 pictures and sold 8. The Gallery was full and the place buzzed with discussions of the groups. There was one dissenter - a journalist who refused to review the show for 'City Life', asking the Curator, 'Who the hell does he think he is? Does he think he's a budding Lowry? They look as if they're walking to Wigan Pier. They're not doing anything'.

John at the Salford exhibition in 1988

John replied that the journalist had seen the point but missed it. Aimlessness is one of his themes. 'It's no good always seeking purpose' - the point was in the pointlessness. Despite the dissenter, the show made John very happy - he felt that he was accepted by the local art establishment and that a wider public was responding to his work.

He was continuously experimenting so that the group series contains great variety. At first he tried to make his figures 'heroic'. He worked in pencil and found that he was continually rubbing out his images as unconsciously he drifted towards an older, working class set of figures

'Modern Tales of Mystery and Imagination'

Despite the bewildering diversity, there are repeated motifs.

Often a central figure makes a supplicatory gesture to the onlookers or supporters. A sweeping, curving arm gives a circular rhythm - making a point in contrast to the more angular outlines of the figures. Sometimes there appears to be consensus - a meeting of minds. In other images there seems to conflict and controversy, disunity rather than solidarity. Are we seeing reconciliation, or debate and argument?

A long queuing line of men may stretch out into the distance, observed by a single figure at the margin. Again there is rhythm and an echo - are these the men who marched away in the Great War, reviewed by an officer? Or are they the unemployed from the waste land of the 1930s, watched by a supercilious foreman in work? The artist seems to be saying, 'Take your pick'.

Like frescos in Italian churches, some groups are overtly religious, the figures framed by the arches of stained glass windows or the entrance to crypts. They may be mitred bishops and saints, or prostitutes and clients. All the groups rely on body language, but the bodies are ambiguous and the language difficult. Are the prostitutes propositioning potential clients, or are the clients themselves making the first move?

Certain groups are angular, abstract and geometrical: a mass of elongated, thin figures in a crowd, all facing to left or right, straight lines punctuated by pin heads.

They can be yellow stick men with red faces, or combine in a cubist pattern of triangular faces and circular, obese bodies. He even ignores the body completely and gives the stick men of a Kandinsky. Some figures are blurred and indistinct, others sharply drawn.

Very few indeed show children, but there are occasional female groups. Again there is ambiguity. Some are openly erotic. Some may be 'on the game': others may just be 'on the razzle'. Perhaps the group images are simply celebrations of the happiness of youth and gaiety, the innocence of inexperience as yet unsoured by the harshness of reality?

John Thompson captures posture and stance instinctively and exactly. His figures process, they stop and talk, they lean forward and back, they face out or have their backs to the viewer, they face to left and right in balance - but whatever their attitude their physicality is precisely captured. Arms point and eyes focus, mouths open or close, the artist conveys emotions of pride, fear or defiance in economic lines. The walker may lurch in hesitant and reticent shuffle, or strut in self-confident swagger. Shoulders may be bent or square, huddled or aggressive. In a pub scene one is not sure what the tap-room customers are actually doing - gesticulating to make a point, or offering to buy another round? Old photographs are transformed by the power of he artist's imagination.

In some groups he tries to capture movement in a figure in a cartoon-like animated technique, a little like the movement in the Bayeux Tapestry. The same figure is seen in different positions. Another motif is taken directly from the cartoon, as the quickly drawn outlines of figures dance balletically or gesture excitedly.

Group Series 49 Mixed Media 20" x 16"
Collection of Michael Dunn

Whilst there are restless experiments - some groups only show torsos, others only heads, some have only a colour wash background, others have street and mill scenes, or seaside postcard images - the constant theme is magic, mystery and metaphor. The group is always enigmatic: men may be fighting or shaking hands in reconciliation: they may be wrestling each other or hugging in emotional reunion.

The figures vary from a dramatic duo or trio in intensive interaction to abstract profiles of disembodied silhouettes.

Colour, tone and texture also vary. Some are sombre and dour in blacks, greys and whites. Some are gay and luminous, as in the stained glass images. Some are smudged and blurred, others striking swirls of bright blues, reds and yellows. There are subtle limes and pinks, and plain backgrounds of white or blue washes. Some are flat like photographs, others have a complex depth. There are often splashes of red to focus attention, or blues, yellows and greens to break monotony.

Group Series 86 *Mixed Media 22" x 30"*
Collection of Charles Barker

25

Group Series 101   *Mixed Media   22" x 26"   Collection of John Thompson*

26

Group Series 116 *Mixed Media 20" x 16"*
Collection of John Buckley

Group Series 138 *Mixed Media 22" x 30"*
Private Collection

28

Group Series 321 *Mixed Media 22" x 26"*
Private Collection

29

Group Series 354 *Mixed Media 22" x 30"*
Collection of Bill Clark

30

Group Series 353 *Oil on Canvas 22" x 18"*
Collection of John Buckley

Group Series 627 *Mixed Media 27" x 20"*
Private Collection

31

Group Series 525 *Mixed Media 20" x 16"*
Private Collection

Group Series 502 *Mixed Media 16" x 12"*
Collection of Charles Barker

Group Series 542 *Mixed Media 22" x 30"*
Private Collection

Group Series 456 *Mixed Media 22" x 30"*
Collection of Claire Curtis-Thomas

Group Series 534 *Mixed Media 22" x 30"*
Collection of Chris Chapman

Group Series 744 *"**Waiting in the Alley**"* *Mixed Media 16" x 12"*
Collection of John Buckley

Group Series 787 *Mixed Media 19" x 15"*
Collection of Charles Barker

Group Series 811 *Mixed Media 22" x 30"*
Collection of John Buckley

Group Series 831 *Mixed Media 22" x 30"*
Collection of John Thompson

Group Series 917 *Mixed Media 20" x 16"*
Private Collection

Group Series 891 *Mixed Media 20" x 16"*
Private Collection

Group Series 750 *Mixed Media 20" x 16"*
Private Collection

Group Series 1198 *Mixed Media 20" x 16"*
Private Collection

Group Series 969
Mixed Media
40" x 30"
Collection of John Thompson

41

Group Series 984 *Mixed Media   16" x 30"*
Private Collection

42

Group Series 1006 *Mixed Media 30" x 22"*
Collection of Mr & Mrs Wood

Group Series 1032 *Mixed Media 30" x 22"*
Collection of Mr & Mrs S Earnshaw

Group Series 1192 *Mixed Media 5" x 22"*
Private Collection

Group Series 835 *Mixed Media 8" x 14"*
Private Collection

Group Series 1196 *Mixed Media   22" x 30"*
Collection of Wendy Momen

Group Series 1210 *Mixed Media 22" x 30"*
Private Collection

Group Series 990 *Mixed Media 30" x 22"*
Collection of John Thompson

Group Series 991 *Mixed Media 30" x 22"*
Collection of John Thompson

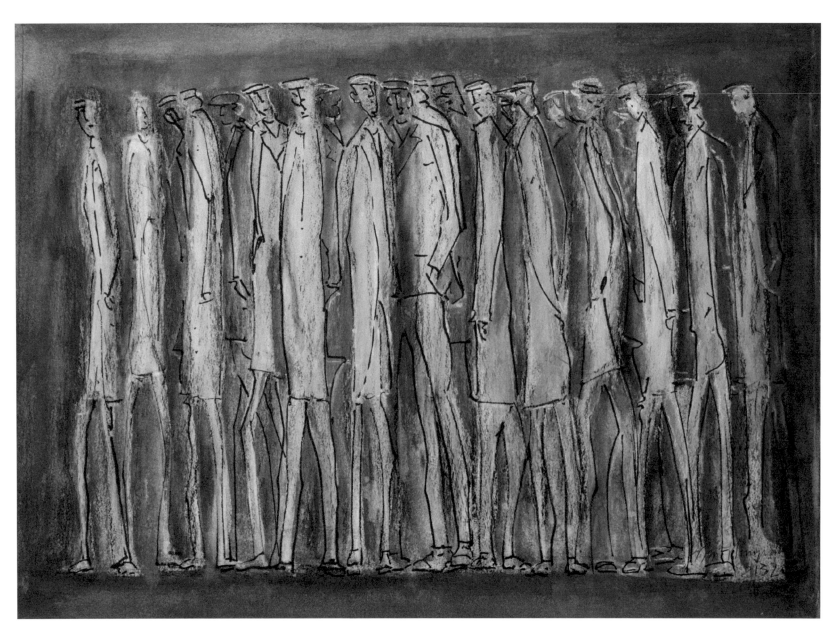

Group Series 2132 *Mixed Media 22" x 30"*
Collection of Bill Clark

Group Series 408 *Mixed Media 30" x 22"*
Collection of John Buckley

Group Series 1090 *Mixed Media 30" x 22"*
Collection of John Thompson

Red Group *Mixed Media 22" x 30"*
Private Collection

An Artistic Range

'I like to do things quickly, immediately, and have it done'.

Techniques

He paints instinctively, using a variety of media: the act of painting is a dance, a movement, a song. He rarely paints on canvas; most of his works are on paper. Marker pens for the groups create spontaneity and confidence in the line. Chalk and charcoal add structure and shape. He may use emulsion paint as background. Oil and water-colours are frequently almost reversible for him. He has more recently become fond of acrylic paints. He will argue that the 'binder' makes the difference to final tones. And of course he is quite willing to use a murky brown wash for his grimy images of the less colourful years 'entre les deux guerres'. Perhaps his technique is best seen as a confident spontaneity and a willingness to break the conventional orthodoxies.

John in his Studio

Portraits and Faces

He loves to experiment in self-portraits - always seeking improvement, if not perfection. His 'Self-portrait with Suit and Tie' is a full-face study in sombre black and blue tones, and subtle shades of light and brown. The expression is severe and serious, the mouth down-turned. The effect is powerful and enigmatic, echoing Rembrandt in its concern with intimations of mortality.

Another intriguing image is the double self-portrait of the good and the bad, the happy and the sad, tied in a Siamese twin circle, by gigantic hands.

Paint and brushes

Although most famous for his groups and figure paintings, John Thompson is a very versatile artist, working in many different genres and styles. He absorbs influences, but is quick to point out that he assimilates rather than borrows.

Double Self Portrait *Watercolour 27" x 22"*
Collection of John Thompson

Self Portrait with Suit and Tie *20" x 16"*
Collection of Maureen Sandiford

He sometimes mischievously introduces himself into a group, the creator in the familiar challenge - ('What do you think of this, then?).

In his search for identity he shifts from the sombre to the confident, from the light to the dark.

Faces are different. Some are monumental and sculpted, reminiscent of the giant heads of Polynesia and Easter Island. Some are blurred and indistinct. Some are clear and sharp - unconscious portraits of neighbours perhaps. Some are like the grotesques of da Vinci. Sad, smiling, snarling, grimacing - the faces reflect a wide gamut of the emotions.

He may play with the faces as Picasso did: mirror images face, like Janus, both ways. ears are mutated into noses.

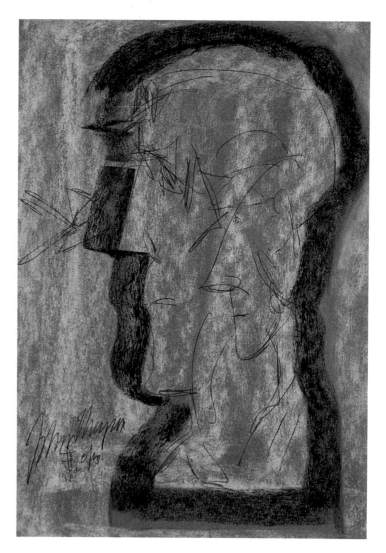

Brown Head *Pastel 16" x 12"*
Private Collection

54

Black Self Portrait *Mixed Media 16" x 12"*
Private Collection

Self Portrait (May 2003) *Mixed Media 16" x 12"*
Private Collection

Head of a Woman *Pastel 9" x 7"*
Collection of John Thompson

Man in Cap *Mixed Media 16" x 12"*
Collection of John Thompson

56

The Sharp Look *Mixed Media 12" x 10"*
Collection of Charles Barker

Group Series 689 *Mixed Media 30" x 22"*
Private Collection

Group 881
Mixed Media
30" x 22"
Collection of
Jo Bennett

58

Group Series No 784 *Mixed Media 30" x 22"*
Private Collection

Group Series No 1019 *Mixed Media 20" x 16"*
Private Collection

Abstracts - surrealism and expressionism

He describes some of his favourite works quite simply - they are unashamedly 'quirky'.

Abstract Head *Mixed Media 15"x11"*
Collection of John Thompson

A surreal influence is often apparent. His figures may be exaggerated and provocative, the colours brash or subtle. The objects in his works give clues to their surroundings - the studio of the artist, the room in the café, the urban street scene. Very often it seems that he is trying to point out both beauty and ugliness in a single image.

Expressionism is seen in his quickly drawn images, a mixture of the funny and the macabre. Sometimes these are nudes, often of African origin. They can be sensuously sexual, and the sexuality carries a threatening quality.

Strangest of all are his abstract, surreal, post-cubist works. Fantasy, dream or nightmare envelop them. Hybrid figures emerge - goat women, circus horses, robotic skeletons. Medieval gargoyles give way to bizarre images of science fiction, compositions of arms, legs, breasts, buttocks. His imagination runs riot in a perverse pleasure at the shock of he new.

Surprise, Surprise
Mixed Media
20" x 16"
Collection John Thompson

That's Magic *Mixed Media 30" x 22"*
Collection of Diane Nobilio

The Worker II *Pastel 20" x 16"*
Collection of Mark Wellburn

Sexaphone *Mixed Media 22" x16"*
Collection of John Thompson

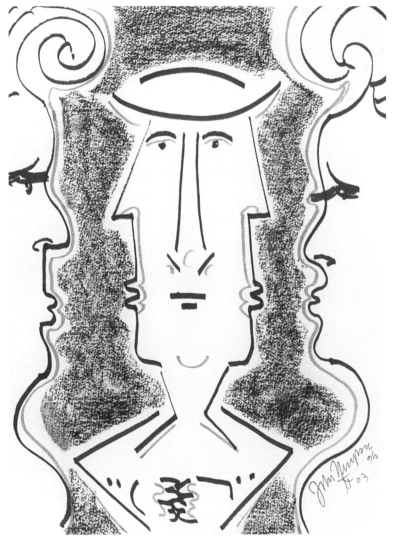

Always *Mixed Media 20" x 16"*
Collection of John Thompson

Together in Separation *Mixed Media 30" x 22"*
Collection of John Thompson

64

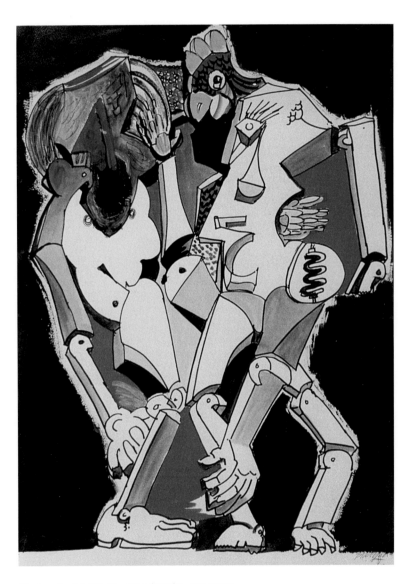

Mechanical Animals *Mixed Media 25" x 18"*
Collection of John Thompson

Egyptians *Mixed Media 16" x 12"*
Collection of John Thompson

Orange Dream *Mixed Media 22" x 30"*
Collection of John Thompson

66

Blue and white abstract *24" x 16"*
Collection of John Thompson

67

Group No 1038 *Mixed Media 30" x 22"*
Private Collection

68

Nude Studies

He is fascinated by the female body. He produced a
number of nude drawings in pencil and pastel. Some of
his nude paintings are traditional: a mature woman
steps out of a bath, in profile and shadow, an echo of
Rembrandt. A nude reclines on a striped sheet, legs
crossed, face turned away and behind her the broad
striped curtains wittily repeat the stripe motif: a white
haired nude figure sits on a couch, back to us: a nude
reclines with raised knees protectively or provocatively:
a frontal view of a young girl, arms akimbo: three nude
girls, one standing and two kneeling - a beautiful
image reminding us of Degas. Such images are erotic
celebrations of beauty.

Some of his nudes are more sinister. Contrasting
colours and ugly, obese physiques hint at both sadness
and sexuality.

Female nude *Pencil Drawing*

These surreal nudes are often grotesque . Their fleshiness, their pendulous breasts and bulging stomachs are almost revolting, in the style of Lucien Freud. Butcher's meat. Lovers kiss in writhing ecstasy. Couples copulate. Two women recline in lesbian poses. A woman stretches her foot towards an exposed backside, as three other nudes observe with pornographic interest. A hand caresses a foot with suggestive undertones.

Perhaps even more unsettling are his abstract nudes. Some are moving and beautiful, as in the mother suckling her baby in classical Madonna and child pose, with curved and flowing lines, but with a Picasso style distortion of the head.

Some are collections of sexual organs - the penis, breasts and nipples, haunches and backsides.

Occasionally the nipples are picked out in red. Again the patterns are distortions as realism gives way to rhythm and simplification and the legs, buttocks, genitals and vaginas are incorporated in disembodied designs. A tangled mass of bodies may be drawn, with arms and legs intertwined. A two headed woman in profile stretches back to touch her heavy breasts with both hands as she stands on muscular legs.

Other abstract nudes show swirling lines of pregnancy. A naked female form takes on the shape of a Henry Moore sculpture. The artist escapes realism in an effort to capture the essence of womanhood. To many his images may be provocative and distasteful, yet his flair and his confidence in his visions, disturbing and distorted though they may be, remain as an impressive reminder of a long European tradition in art.

Blond Nude *Pastel 30" x 22"*
Collection of Diane Nobilio

Standing Nude *Pastel 12" x 8"*
Collection of John Thompson

71

Nemesis *Mixed Media 29" x 29" Collection of John Thompson*

72

Dark Orange
Mixed Media
30" x 22"
Collection of
John Thompson

Languish
Mixed Media
30" x 22"
Collection of
John Thompson

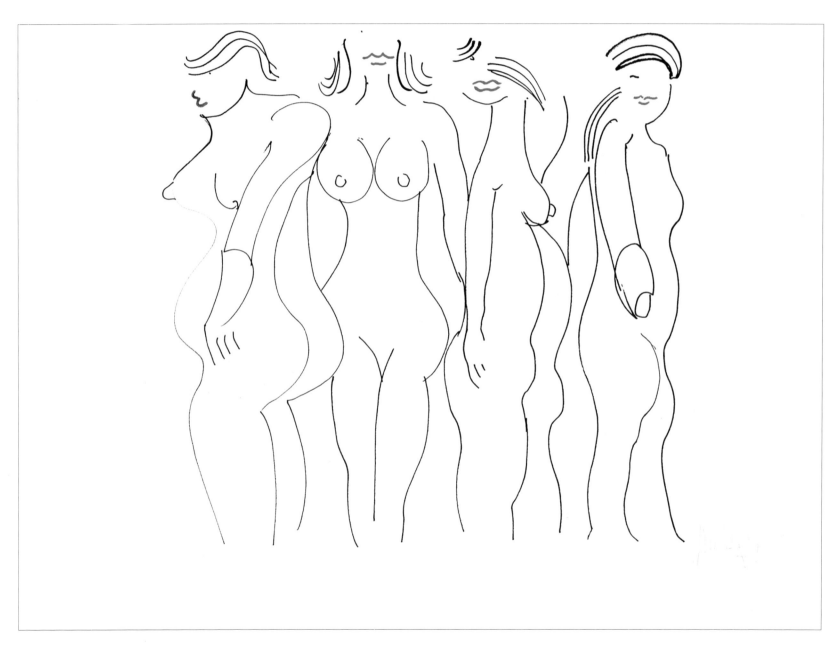

Hot Lips *Felt Pen 22" x 30"*
Collection of John Thompson

Blusome *Mixed Media 22" x 30"*
Collection of John Thompson

76

The Other side of JT *Mixed Media 32" x 23"*
Collection of John Thompson

Pink Ladies *Mixed Media 20" x 16"*
Collection of John Thompson

77

Rain at Llanberis - Detail

Landscape and Townscape

Landscapes and townscapes were his staple at first and they also vary enormously in style, from the traditional images of rural idyll to the more impressionistic townscapes. He is often not so much interested in realism as in atmosphere. His may be a bird's eye view, a reminder of a vanished age or of the links between town and country.

This search for mood and tone leads him from pastoral landscapes with Corot-like trees

Cornish Fishing Boats *Mixed Media 8" x 16"*
Collection of John Thompson

bending in the wind, to more impressionistic images of villages and seaside. An early sketchbook is full of images painted during a holiday in North Wales, "I forgot my camera so I bought some paints and painted what I saw"

Landscape with Trees *Pastel*

His street scenes are industrial, with mills and factories, smoking chimneys and shadowy figures. He enjoys hinting at such urbanisation in the background to some of his groups.

Paintings from a trip to Wales

Beach and sea 1 *Oil on Paper 7" x 9"*
Collection of John Thompson

Beach and Sea 2 *Oil on Paper 7" x 9"*
Collection of John Thompson

Welsh Valley Scene *Oil on Paper 7" x 9"*
Collection of John Thompson

Dinas Dinlle *Oil on Paper 7" x 9"*
Collection of John Thompson

Smoking Chimneys *Pastel*

The finding of beauty in apparent ugliness has a long history: one thinks of Valette, Lowry, Monet and Derain. Perhaps the novelist, Henry Green, expressed this clearly in his eccentric style in his 1929 novel, 'Living':

'Town beneath them was a deep blue, like the Gulf Stream, with channels which were the roads cutting it up, appearing, being hidden, and they the colour of steel when it has been machined. Above it factory chimneys were built, the nearest rose up from the level of where they were in bedroom only way away, and others away came not so high. Rain had fallen ninety minutes before and this wet was now drying off the roofs. But these still glowed with white cold that steel has when it has been machined, and the streets also'.

Sunset *Mixed Media 12" x 16"*
Collection of John Thompson

John Thompson's landscapes try to capture a tactile sense of power and mystery, in images of both beauty and squalor..

Arundel *Watercolour 16" x 12³/₄"*
Collection of John Thompson

Delph, Saddleworth *Watercolour 22" x 14"*
Collection of John Thompson

Man in Street *Oil on Canvas 30" x 20"*
Collection of John Thompson

Werneth Plate Layers and Snowy 1939
Mixed Media 16" x 13" Collection John Thompson

Rhodes Bank Oldham *Mixed Media 11" x 15"*
Collection of Maureen Sandiford

84

Group Series 1201 *22" x 30"*
Private Collection

Oldham Market *Mixed Media 15" x 19"*
Collection of Maureen Sandiford

Group Series 1167 *Mixed Media 30" x 22"*
Private Collection

Group Series 836 *Mixed Media 30" x 22"*
Private Collection

Group 1129 *Mixed Media 16" x 12"*
Collection of John Thompson

Burn Bank *Mixed Media 30" x 20*
Collection of John Thompson

Birmingham
Mixed Media
30" x 22"
Collection of
John Thompson

Flower Painting and Still Life

John with an early Still Life Painting

Another traditional genre which engages him is flower painting. Again it is not the delicate detail which is his concern but the emotional impact of the image. Perhaps this common tradition enables him to address his central theme of transience, of constant change and impermanence.

Yet the flower images are by no means obsessed with *vanitas*. He is much more involved in shape, pattern, rhythm and colour. The pots are sturdy, often striped, and the flowers burst into pointilliste explosions. Once more it is mood and expression that he captures - he simplifies the image and the flower becomes a symbol of happiness or sadness, of fertility or barrenness.

His palate may be harsh or subtle, the images abstract or realistic, the vases conventional or distorted.

His still lifes continue this search for a modern idiom. Tables are seen from above, they lean, the fruit on them threatens to spill onto the floor. He works with blocks of colour. Three bottles and a glass, kitchen utensils hanging on a wall - simple conceptions cleverly woven into a warm ensemble. Furniture with gaily coloured cushions face the open window with the sea beyond - echoes of Matisse and Christopher Wood.

Irisies *Mixed Media 22" x 30"*
Collection of John Thompson

Memories *Mixed Media 19" x 15"*
Collection of John Thompson

The Studio, Upper Mill *Mixed Media 20" x 16"*
Collection of John Thompson

92

Cezanne Flowers
Oil on Canvas
20" x 16"
Collection of John Thompson

Flowers on an Orange Background *Mixed Media 19" x 15"*
Collection of John Buckley

Basket of Fruit *Pastel 30" x 22"*
Collection of John Thompson

94

Blue and White Flowers *Mixed Media 30" x 22"*
Collection of John Thompson

Bottles *Mixed Media 23" x 14"*
Collection of John Thompson

Black and Whites

John shows his mischievousness in a series of cartoon- like 'matchstick' figures, quickly sketched in miniature versions of his groups. His captions are ironical and witty, often poking fun at contemporary fashions and foibles. The balance is exact and the humour succinct.

A group of men in a queue are almost punctuated by the short skirt of a single woman. Some lean back, others forward, most are tall but one is short. The more one looks the more rhythm one sees.

Another simple image shows a receding group of women, one holding the hand of a child. The path snakes towards a distant wood and village - but where are they going? To church? To work? To school? The grey background gives the drawing a cold and frosty feeling.

An image like a wood block shows figures in angular poses, facing each other, the background roughly cross hatched. It is a stylish, almost stylised image.

Run for Cover *Felt Pen 5" x 20"*
Private Collection

"I could swear it was this way" Felt Pen 5" x 7"

Shopping Felt Pen 5" x 7"

Group 914 Felt Pen 11" x 15"

The Queue Felt Pen 6" x 13"

Group 2145 *Felt Pen 12" x 10"*

The new arrival.

The New Arrival *Felt Pen 12" x 9"*

Group 1204 - Dissertation   *Charcoal and Pencil 22" x 30"*
Private Collection

99

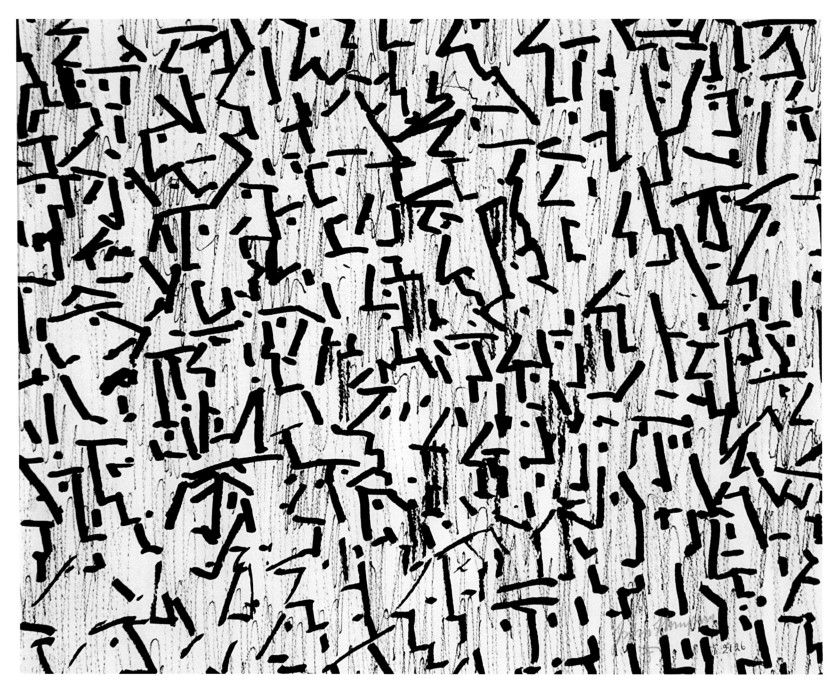

Group 2126   *Felt Pen and watercolour 16" x 20" Private Collection*

100

Group 1112 *30" x 22"*

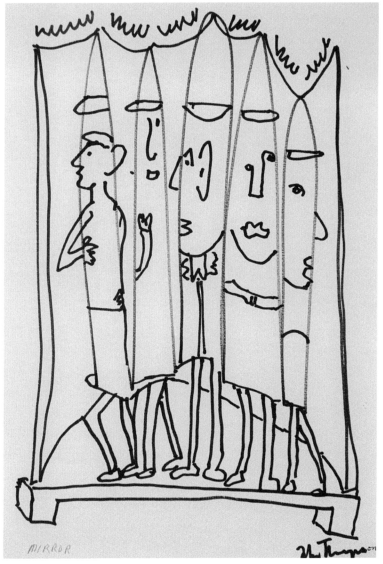

Mirror *Felt Pen 12" x 8"*

Why Are We Waiting *Felt Pen 8" x 10"*

Cloth Cap Concerto *Felt Pen 7" x 5"*

Friends and Collectors

'Some can see and understand what I am doing'.

John has a loyal following of dedicated friends and collectors. As Jo Bennett said, buying his work is addictive. If John has not yet quite reached cult status, some of his friends collect his work with religious fervour.

Charles Barker

His first serious patron was Charles Barker, a civil servant, now working in Sefton, Liverpool, the Director of Social Services. Charlie's impressive suite of offices is packed with contemporary paintings - a refreshing contrast in their light and colour to those usually grey citadels of drab bureaucracy. He is an incisive and decisive Scotsman to whom art collecting is a passion - a passion first inflamed by John's work. When Charlie worked at Stalybridge he would come in to the Alexandra Craft Centre every week and the red stickers would multiply. John's experience in retail led him to try to make his work always 'affordable', even if that meant accepting payments in instalments. Charlie

admired his work - he found it evocative, stimulating and funny. He made friends with this most approachable of painters, sympathised with his streak of anti-establishment idiosyncrasies, and built up a collection of over one hundred of his paintings, a valuable guide to his stylistic evolution. Charlie is the proud owner of Group Series No 1 and has selected this as his favourite painting as it reminds him of his grandfather.

Group Series G1 *Mixed Media 20" x 16"*
Collection of Charles Barker

Jenny Knight

Another great collector is Jenny Knight. After an unhappy start to their friendship, when her husband, Martin, was turned out of the Craft Centre and told not to darken his door again, Jenny found in John a shaft of enlightenment and civilisation in the frozen north. She is a West Sussex girl by birth, and had found it hard to adjust to life in Lancashire at first. She found in John's paintings and his character an expression of the dourness and the desperation of the depression of the inter-war years. The power and strength of his groups, the clever use of light and colour, the complex stances and attitudes of these apparently living men gave her goose pimples, and she had to begin collecting. They were the key to a different country for her. Many of his group paintings are hung in their renovated farmhouse near Albi in the south of France.

Her favourite painting is a group of angular figures in a brown background, with small heads and triangular feet. With their long jackets they could be teddy-boys. The work has a strong sense of rhythm and counter rhythm.

Group Series No 937 *Mixed Media 22" x 30"*
Collection of Mrs Jenny Knight

John Buckley

John Buckley, a local businessman, is a more recent collector. Five years ago he passed the studio with his wife and daughter and struck up an immediate friendship.

Marie, his daughter, bought the first painting (the dramatic 'Three Generations'), and he now has over fifty of John's works, covering a wide range from groups to flowers and still lifes. They remind him of an earlier family history, of his grandfather and the hungry thirties, the flat cap and the woodbine images. John was also new to the world of art collecting, and it was John Thompson who opened his eyes to pictures and taught him elements of appreciation. The personal link with the artist and the studio means a great deal to John Buckley - he loves the wit and humour and the understanding that stems from friendship. He is proud of the fact that, 'I virtually watch him paint them - I buy them before they've dried'. His favourite painting is an atmospheric group scene, he loves the use of light in the painting

Group Series No 1143 *30" x 22"*
Collection of John Buckley

105

Claire Curtis-Thomas

The Liverpool MP Mrs Claire Curtis-Thomas is also a serious collector. One of his more voluptuous nude scenes creates conversation in her dining room. Charlie Barker first introduced her to his work and she was quick to appreciate his ability to strip away the irrelevant and focus on the essence of a subject.

She regards many of the groups as echoes of an urban past. She also admires his spontaneity and improvisation. She was instrumental in getting his work accepted by the House of Lords.

Her favourite painting is a very dark, intense painting of a man, it's a very powerful painting and is unlike any other John Thompson she has seen.

Dark Man *Oil on Paper 30" x 22"*
Collection of Claire Curtis-Thomas

Colin Frost, Julia Cox and Maureen Sandiford

Colin Frost and Julia Cox have collected his work since meeting him in the studio in 1992. They were captivated by his images and fascinated by his conversation. After four hours of discursive discussion, they bought the first of their present collection of almost fifty paintings - an extremely catholic selection. They both admire his vibrant use of colour, the abstract angularity of some of his figures, and the precision of his drawing. They love the way his work keeps its ability to surprise and shock and marvel that familiarity never breeds contempt. Once again his patrons have become almost part of his family, as they even sacrifice holidays for art.

Julia's favourite work is a group in blue. Anonymous figures with angular bodies and the familiar cloth caps react in a confusing mixture of heads, legs and arms, wearing a mosaic of patchwork clothes. It is a shadowy and haunting image.

Their friend Maureen Sandiford is also a keen collector. She is captivated by his sense of humour and his warm sensitivity. As a businesswoman she admires his canny salesmanship - 'You don't know John is selling you a picture until you have bought it!'. She is amazed at the diversity of his work and thinks that he improves with age - like cheese, the older he gets, the higher he gets? She is drawn towards his empathetic and atmospheric pictures of working life in Manchester.

Group Series No 822 *Mixed Media 30" x 22"*
Collection of Julia Cox

107

Group Series No 221
The Grand Rouge
Mixed Media
22" x 30
Collection of Colin Frost

Group Series No 863
Mixed Media
22" x 30"
Collection of
Maureen Sandiford

Giulio and Diane Nobilio

Giulio and Diane Nobilio have many of his pictures in their house in an Italian village. Diane has collected his work for over eighteen years. She first met him at the Alexandra Craft Centre where he was painting - his wife Shirley sitting by his side. Diane was immediately struck by the power of his images - they had the 'wow' factor. She immediately knew that she wanted to own some of John's work, though she was new to art collecting. When she talked to him she was hooked by his character as well as his painting. Forty-odd pictures later and she is still collecting, still listening to his marathon stories. His work is affordable and he is approachable.

Diane speaks with a bubbling enthusiasm about the range of his work, and with an authoritative understanding of his concerns, stemming from many hours of listening as a friend and patron. 'Bold, dramatic and powerful' - that is her verdict on his instant impact.

Diane's favourite work is also a group - painted in oil. The grey figures contrast with a robust red background. Their shoes are black. Their gestures are expressive. They could be poseurs - or a threatening gang?

Group 1163 *Mixed Media 22" x 30"*
Collection of Diane and Giulio Nobilio

Chris Chapman

Chris has been a great help to John - at times a godsend. He has a deep knowledge of art and art history and quickly appreciated the originality and the vitality of his work. He introduced him to Henry Donn, with his Gallery in Whitefield, who proved to be a valuable outlet, and Chris also organised an exhibition at the Blyth Gallery in Manchester. His shrewd entrepreneurial gifts gave John the stamina to survive leaner times after his move to Kinders Lane, and the courage to wait for wider recognition.

One of Chris's favourite works is a vividly coloured pastel depicting a comical looking man dressed all in white reaching out to pet a white dog.

Oldham Wakes *Pastel 20" x 16"*
Collection of Chris Chapman

Michael Dunn

Michael Dunn is a retired businessman and keen photographer. He has been buying John's work since 1987. He particularly likes an early Group Series painting which he bought in 1988, it shows a group of light figures against a black background. He has become a good friend over the years, at one stage John was considering abandoning the Group paintings but Michael encouraged him to carry on. He has many of John's early Group Series paintings, a number of which were bought at John's exhibition at Salford Art Gallery in 1988. He particularly likes one painting which has a series of light coloured men against a stark black background.

Group Series 113 Mixed Media 22" x 30"
Collection of Michael Dunn

Bill Clark

Bill Clark now represents John Thompson and is co-author of this book. His favourite painting is a classic group series painting, it consists of 10 men all looking in different directions against a light background. This painting has special significance because it was a present from John Thompson and will be treasured forever.

Group Series No 1195 *Mixed Media 22" x 30"*
Collection of Bill Clark

Cosmopolitan

On the back of a 1998 abstract nude John listed his international sales - to Marseilles, Luxembourg, the Austrian Tyrol, Coburg, New Zealand, South Africa, Australia, the USA (Quaker Hill, California, Dallas), Holland, Brazil, Singapore, Toronto, Jersey, Munich - and of course, Stalybridge!

John is delighted by his burgeoning reputation. He certainly appreciates the appreciation. As Diane Nobilio points out he is still genuinely astounded at the lengths people will go to own one of his works, and can't quite believe how much his friends and collectors value his unique talents.

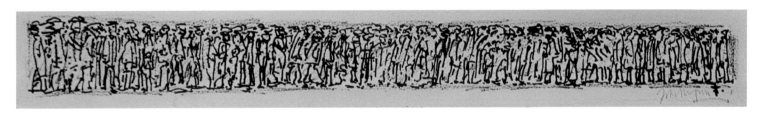

The Line *Felt Pen 3" x 21"*
Private Collection

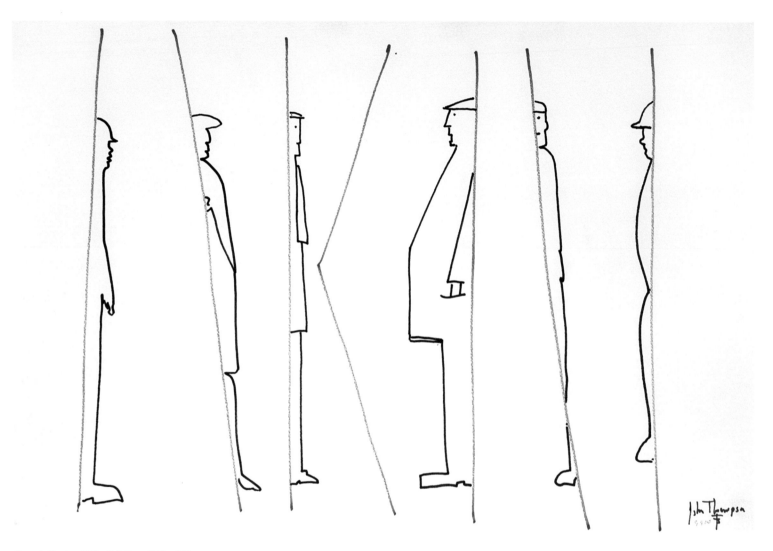

Group Series 900 *Felt Pen 22" x 30"*
Private Collection

114

Conclusion

'I like to read what artists say, rather than see what they've done'

For many years he avoided the study of other great painters for fear of being too overtly influenced. Yet he is very much aware of the great tradition and speaks penetratingly of the work of El Greco, Rembrandt, Daumier, Matisse, Rodin, Picasso, Kandinsky, Miro, Dali, and Bacon - amongst many.

He can paint 'in the style of' with great fertility and facility, but he strives to keep his own style, his own idiom - an idiom which is confident and contemporary.

Types of ambiguity: uses of imagination.

The perils of subjective interpretation should be obvious. There is a famous story of Lillian Browse, doyenne of the London art world between the wars. She was organising the sale of a Stanley Spencer drawing, and she confidently told the artist what the theme of the work really was. 'What a very nice thought', Spencer said calmly. 'It never occurred to me'. And so with John Thompson. When you proffer an opinion, his usual response is, 'Do you think so?'

He is a painter of ideas, but he also expresses moods, emotions and sentiment. He may use traditional forms, yet he searches continuously to transform them. He loves to experiment. He strives for originality through the imaginative expression of ambiguities. His work shuns indifference and craves a response, be it of sympathy or denial.

He would doubtless agree with Monet who wrote in old age: 'I have painted for half a century...but far from decreasing, my sensitivity has sharpened with age...I have nothing to fear from old age as long as constant contact with the outside world keeps up my curiosity and my hand remains the quick and faithful servant of my perception'.

Men in The Pink   *Mixed Media   8" x 6"*
Private Collection

Even more fitting are the words of Dürer in his 'Nourishment for Young Painters' of 1508. A good artist he argued always has more to express:

'if it were possible that he lived forever, his inner ideas...would always give him something new to express through his works'.

Children, such as the five- year old girl Ellie Moorhouse from Royton, his youngest collector, respond to this 'painter man' in awed fascination. She shyly presents him with one of her own drawings of a snowman ('she is always drawing'), and John reciprocates with a quick sketch of a group with a dog. Always something new...

In the case of John Thompson, we must be grateful that the springs of creativity still burst forth so strongly.

Appendix

John does go in for something completely different from time to time. His poetry is full of Lancashire hills and valleys, of nostalgia for a lost past, of the simple celebration of 'emotion recollected in tranquillity'. In its incisive brevity it is most reminiscent of the Japanese haiku.

Here are some examples:-

A Selection of verse - the other side of John Thompson.

Towards Winter

Waving hands goodbye to summer

Coloured days in grey depart

Mornings pale uncertain coming

Chills the day and stills the lark

Once the summers gentle evening

Clothed the laughter in the park

Now the leaves of life are flying

Past the windows in the dark

~ ~ ~

Autumn of 56 years (1980)

Sadness blows each leaf

I was your summer

I floated on more

Confident and gentle winds

Forgive me if I am now frail

My brother fell yesterday

We wait we wait

Frailer now

You will remember me

Won't you?

~ ~ ~

Rain

Umbrella headed folk
Disappear in rain and smoke
Windows washed with wetted
Weather
Bring the hills and sky together

~ ~ ~

Old Photographs

Smiles like frozen songs
Eyes in faces fading
Still and staring
Sunlit wands pinned in cobwebs
Drying like paper

~ ~ ~

Armistice Day

On Sundays cold November day
A secret calling through the mists
Of bells and bells in dour remembrance
Come back - come back your
Marching still
In this cold and awful chill

Through the Window
October 16th 1996

Raindrops on the telephone wire
Run like soldiers
Steadily and evenly and one by
One fall
With a graceful inevitability

Chronology

1924	Born at Malta Street, Salem, Oldham
1938	Left school, aged fourteen
1939	Designed a stand for the British Empire Exhibition
1940s	Worked on the railways
1950s	Worked in retail
1955	Marriage to Shirley
1960s-70s	Display Manager in Furniture stores
1980	Began career as an independent artist, aged fifty-six. Set up studio in The Alexandra Craft Centre.
1981	Engagement portrait of Charles and Diana
1986	The first in the great series of Group paintings
1988	First one man exhibition at Salford Art Gallery
1988	Exhibited at Rochdale Art Gallery
1990,91,94	Exhibited at the Royal Watercolour Exhibition, London
1993,94	Exhibited at the Barn Gallery, Manchester
1999	Moved to present studio, Kinders Lane, Greenfield
2001	Exhibited at the Blyth Gallery, Manchester
2002	Exhibited at the Gallery, Manchester's Art House
2002	Three paintings chosen to hang in the House of Lords' Collection
2004	Retrospective at the Gallery, Manchester's Art House, to celebrate his eightieth birthday.
2005	Represented by Bill Clark of Clark Art Ltd.
Collections	House of Lords: many substantial private British and international collections.